Falling
Out of
the Sky

Falling
Out of
the Sky

poems

Deborah Pope

Louisiana State University Press
Baton Rouge 1999

Designer: Michele Myatt Quinn
Typeface: Bembo
Printer and binder: Edwards Brothers, Inc.

Library of Congress Cataloging-in-Publication Data

Pope, Deborah.
      Falling out of the sky: poems / Deborah Pope.
          p.   cm.
      ISBN 0-8071-2359-5 (cloth: alk. paper). —ISBN 0-8071-2360-9
      (pbk.: alk. paper)
          I. Title.
      PS3566.0625F35   1999
      811'.54—dc21   98-51115
                                                                          CIP

Grateful acknowledgment is made to the authors of the following periodicals, in
which some of the poems herein first appeared: *Calyx, Carolina Quarterly, Georgia Re-
view, Literary Review, Poet & Critic, Poetry, Poetry Northwest, Prairie Schooner, Shenandoah,
Southern Humanities Review, Southern Poetry Review, Southern Review, TriQuarterly.*
      "Plainspoken" appeared originally in *The Store of Joys,* edited by Huston Paschal
(John Blair, 1997).

The paper in this book meets the guidelines for permanence and durability of the
Committee on Production Guidelines for Book Longevity of the Council on Library
Resources. ∞

This publication is supported in part by a grant from the National Endowment for the Arts.

for NICHOLAS and MATTHEW

Contents

I

I

Age. How to think of it.
Time between *not yet*
and *never again,*
between the *mezzo piano*
and the *mezzo forte.*

Thinking ahead   *what haven't I done*
to the next   *what haven't I done*
through the decades and the door
that opens suddenly on space,
time like a mechanical stair
unstoppably moving,
its metal mouth biting
the treads off, shutting
the lights off
closer and closer.

I had expected more perspective,
I had expected more calm,
more of the dusk-lit *fermata*
of reflection, I suppose.
To know whom and what I loved
seemed little enough to ask.
I looked for more permanence
in these matters.
I am surprised, looking back,
how easily some things fell away.
I am surprised, looking back,
how much the doing of one thing
was the not-doing of another.

I had thought my desires,
like clever children's toys,
would be self-correcting
and age-appropriate.
I had thought the choices
would be clearer,
that there would be more of them,
that when I came to those
forecast utensils in the road,
the trails would be cut,
signposts appear,
and the implements would be as predicted,
not the rusted cleaver I found.
I thought I would have some answers,
and I do, but for nothing
I am ever asked.

Where is the pattern
time promised to disclose,
the tapestry, mural,
the steady accretion of design?
It is all so partial,
so improvised,
only pieces of things, scraps
awaiting their shape and dreaming
that fate, like an old country doctor,
is somewhere still lugging his remedies
and tincture-pouch of possibles.

An angel has begun to speak to me,
a fact it is wise to avoid mentioning
in therapeutic situations.

She is kind but direct with me,
now hectoring, now forgiving,
delivering her lessons of mercy and voice.
I am grateful when she comes,
a long-distance caller, my foreign correspondent,
startling me in my head
like a roadwork sign
scrolling and alerting
bridge out   lanes narrow
signalman ahead.

Sometimes I think I am growing invisible,
becoming the color of air.
People, seasons, ownings
more and more pass through me.
I am lighter than I have ever been,
more foolish, more longing,
wrong about so much.
I did not know I could possibly feel
as if nothing had happened yet,
as if it were only now beginning,
breath rising, eyes lifting,
fingers opening for their first
wondering touch of the world.

We live in a house of glass.
It is spring and the time
of birds flying rashly
into our windows.
They hit, thump hard,
then drop, unmoving,
in the grass.

Some are only stunned.
Later when we come
dully with the shovel,
they have gone.
The rest break their necks.
Sometimes you cannot tell
which is which.

What do they see,
some cunning of green,
a ghostly beguiling
so oddly twin?
Some beacon they imagine
they can harmlessly
steer toward

in that clearing
just through there
before the sudden world
steps between?
I don't know on which side
more folly falls,
or what those who rise

carry back with them
into the sky.
We all ambush ourselves
at borders thin but absolute,
and go forever marked
by what we see,
or failed to.

after Georgia O'Keeffe's
Cebolla Church, 1937

I

Again we are struck
as always in O'Keeffe
by absence,

the absolute lack
of the need
for us.

II

More barn than benefice,
these low walls slope
in unbroken sun,

the maize-colored stone shimmers
like a ripe crop
out of the dirt around it.

Clouds draw thin white wakes
across an infinite-seeming blue.
Involuntarily

even at this remove
we squint against such light
unbidden, unrelieved.

Sealed against us,
against revealings,
a sublime sufficiency

unto itself.
It is our own need we meet.
This is the church at Cebolla.

III

Used to invitation,
the necessary consequence
of our gaze,

we sift for easy signs,
slowly noting
the vacant air—

two sightless, blue-black windows,
a shut side door.
Portals we might have sought

are turned and imaginary.
No higher than the roof's pitch,
a wry suggestion of buttress

in the shadow,
rise perpendicular sticks
slivered almost to invisibility—

a thin limning of cross.
Cebolla meaning bulb,
meaning onion—

enclosed, common,
of the earth.
And like an onion

there is no clear way
to enter here.
Agarrar la cebolla

to seize power, they say
in the tongue of this place
where layers of light,

sand-wind, and time
know something
of power.

Come by way
of the hard, flat field,
come to the unmarked door,

come barefoot and wait
without intentions
under the sun.

Ponder the name
of the place,
of the object

you have carried here,
plain, mysterious,
in your hands,

no beginning and no end,
Cebolla meaning power,
meaning onion.

This is how the sacred happens.

MOTHER-RIGHT

> Sons branch out,
> but one woman leads to another.
> —Margaret Atwood

Whatever truth is,
it comes finished.
So that sometimes in the small
quiet of the dark, or still
of summer afternoon,
a kind of horizonless calm comes,
when I see through years
like clear water, and say,
it is true, it is so,
she loved me badly.
I can say it
without anger, emptiness,
agitation of arrangements,
I can say it
like a fact I need
do nothing about,
a thing simply there
like a legend on a picture
that I read on a wall
in the museum of days.
At such times I feel wise,
vivid, oracular,
I feel patient at failure,
proud of the absence of blame.
And I step forth
as if from the cool
of that dusty vestibule,
a foyer back into the light
of a day where I see

my own children running,
arms stretched,
their elongated, arrowing shadows
wincing my heart,
a step before they do.

BAD CHILD

He says he wishes I was not
even living, he says he wishes
I would go away,
swinging his small fists at me,
his shirt with spilled milk
still dripping, his arms
two jerking propellers
of fury and shame.
I am wiping at milk on the couch,
the dashed basin it is making,
saying milk of all things,
the smell, the stain, how
can you be so clumsy, careless,
running through my spiral
of tirade toward everything
so shabby, used, nobody cares,
no one looks after things
in this house and can't you
even say you're sorry?
He skulks in the hall,
making sure I can hear
how he hates me.
I clamp shut not to yell
I hate you back, rigid
with fatigue, the unspilled
angers of the house.
It is not good to tell children
you hate them, but they go on
yelling and yelling it,
somewhere their father
saying wearily that's enough.
It is no good to go

in when he's sleeping,
to smooth his red face,
his ribs just under the skin
like two hands reaching up
through water, too late
to lean down in the dark,
breathe close the damp hair,
the pool of milk and skin,
croon I'm sorry,
sorry, sorry.

Pantoum for a Child in Fall

A boy is running, he is my son—
I see his slender back, the wind-stroked hair—
this is the scene I want to remember,
such abandon of body, the headlong joy.

I see his slender back, the wind-stroked hair
through a glitter of leaves in the air,
such abandon of body and headlong joy
floating like motes in a snow-globe.

The glitter of leaves in the air
outnumbers the years we will have,
floating like motes in a snow-globe,
gold feathering over the moment's tableau.

Outnumbering the years we will have
are the summoning trees in the forest,
gold feathering over the moment's tableau.
Already receding, he grows smaller.

The summoning trees in the forest
root to the earth, trace the dome of sky.
Already receding, he grows smaller,
when he disappears,

rooted to earth, tracing the dome of sky,
I will turn this globe over in my hand.
When he disappears,
I will hold his wild career of light

and turn this globe over in my hand—
this is the scene I want to remember.
I will hold his wild career of light.
A boy is running, he is my son.

After all this time
I still dream
how it might have worked
though you will never come back
and with reason
and I would never go back
and with reason.
Still. Still.
Again I build up the woodstove
and go out to look at the stars.
Our years now are just
that dark, remote,
and strung with just
such scattered,
inexplicable light.

THE WOMAN QUESTION

after Frederick Frieseke's
The Garden Parasol, 1907

I shift to take you in
against the settled poise of the day,
a shadow over the chinoiserie.

Your fingers bracelet my wrist,
your lips touch along my skin
like stops along a flute.

I keep the place in my book
and close my eyes, tired
of the way your gaze grazes my face.

You stroke along the prop of my ankle,
think taking small nips
in my neck will arouse me.

It is an irritant to shape these sounds
and float them back to you
across a pool of pleasantries.

It is not enough
you look at me so, you sink
beside my chair, begin to speak,

apologize, you cannot help it,
you say, I am so beautiful.
Have you never noticed

how you repeat yourself?
Listen to the wind
in the lush summer leaves,

their sound is a rush of water,
a licking of flame. Feel
how this late sun spreads its stain

across the skin like sticky honey.
Above cool throats, the purpled lips
of iris are beginning to part.

I will just loosen this pearl.

Exotic Nights at the Savoy; or, a Brief History of British Imperialism

"I remember Daddy walking to work
under the yellow umbrella,"
sang one of the three
"dangerously beautiful" daughters
of the third white Rajah of Sarawak.
"It was a magical place, a dream,"
trilled out her sisters,
Princess Gold, Princess Pearl.
In the sun-drunk market were pawpaws,
orchids, baskets of jackfruit
and mahi, swirls of bright
bodies, petals of batik,
while up the smooth, cinnamon fingers
of rivers blurred legends
of Khayam, Nyang, Malay,
and the long houses of lumber camps.

Lord over all in Istang,
in his palace of marble and wicker,
their father wove absolute power,
the doze of life or death.
It was said the first white Rajah,
Legendary Soldier, Conqueror of Borneo,
had a fine figure, wore a glass eye,
and spoke mostly, if badly, in French.
At state dinners he urinated
over balconies. A duchess once
thought it was raining.
The second white Rajah left his Ranee

for long trips up the Rijang,
took tribal names, native dress,
departed only to die in Surrey.

The last white Rajah, stiff
and correct, had his wife select
his young mistresses,
sold his freehold to England
at the first snarl of war,
went home and hung blowguns in the den.
And the fatally lovely princesses
waltzed off, one with a jockey,
one with a gent, and one with a Yankee
bandman who crooned,
O Sarawacky, my Sarawacky,
under the green bamboo, bamboo,
and the dark suits swayed,
the ivory arms glimmered,
and a land lay small and flat
as a child's drawing, with trees
like kindling, rivers like rakes,
hollows for faces,
and the fat, yellow sun
hanging down like a spider.

THE CITY OF HEAVEN

for Roger Manley,
   who first photographed the City of Heaven

Joshua Stewart of Syllable, Georgia,
stood out on his front porch one July
watching an eighteen-wheeler fly over,
circle three times,
and land in his soybean field.
A truck-driving angel heaved down,
burly and rough.
He knew it was an angel
because it had wings.
He knew it was the driver
because he had a tattoo.
And the angel told Joshua,
The Lord has a plan for you.
He said, Build me the City of Heaven.
Then the angel said, I'll come back
to check what you've done,
and if I like what I see
I'll give you everything
in this truck.

Joshua knew he must do what the Lord
had commanded, but poor as he was
he had nothing to build
the City of Heaven with.
All he had was his shack, the land,
and a clearing in back
where folks had tossed trash
and cans for years out of memory.
So Joshua went down, looked around,

and found he was rich in one thing,
and so he began to build
his city from tin.

He raised up in the fields
a tin-can grocery, a tin-can café,
the main street and city hall,
a YMCA. He worked without rest,
every minute he could spare,
built everything life-size,
big enough to walk around in.
Until at last he ran out of cans,
and became afraid for the time
when the angel would return.
And he did. And he said,
Joshua, the answer is simple—
if you want more cans,
you must plant them.
so Joshua did as he was told,
and planted his cans,
sowed them like seeds,
tilled them like grain
in the rust-colored dirt,
he hung cans from branches
of trees in the orchard,
on the fences of fields,
and he watered them,
and tended them,

and the earth and the fields
rewarded his labors,
they gave and gave,

every time he walked out
he gathered more cans,
reaping the furrows and vines,
culling the ditches and fallows
and gullies by the road
where they heaped in the old hedges
and leaped the slow-moving washes,
all sizes and shapes,
silvered and knuckled,
pleated and petaled, abloom
in rainbows of colors,
going wild, fertile
a hundredfold over,
rising their sure
and shining way
toward heaven.

Cura Animarum Outside Canaan, West Virginia

A thin pelt of winter trees
bristles the rim of hills,
encircles the frost-crimped fields,
crosscut by creeks
in their slow, black honey
and the echoing cord of road.
In the distance, a solitary combine
churns its givens of earth,
the skeletal wheel clutching
late corn in under the sky's milky lid.
Husks of teasel and rusted candles
of sumac choke the deep washes
where scrub pines jut like mealy drumsticks.
In a clearing, beside a residue
of sheds, whitewashed stones
spell carefully out   *Repent.*
Beyond, a low dwindle of stones
descends a family slope
before they fall from sight
in the next turn, and the next,
the hollows closing,
disclosing, in a flung rag
of birds, the untracked veer
of our way.

II

It was just past five
on a Thursday in October,
before the clocks had changed
and the leaves had fallen.
It was just after
the storm had passed.
It was coming on evening,
coming on dark,
the hour of lamps and kitchens,
before we were seated
and facing each other.
There was a light
all around the house,
it was rising
from the bent-back grass
and the dripping trees,
from the carved sky
and luminous surfaces
of the room,
the children were moving
quietly to the windows,
they were standing there
encircled, calling
to us where we were
already watching—
all suspended
in sudden, time-rinsed
transparency—
wanting to hold
before it was gone
such accidental, possessable
gold   gold.

THE CALL

The phone slices into
the bright rind of the kitchen,
where I stand rinsing lettuce,
my youngest plunking plates down
on the table. In the din,
a doctor is saying something,
it has clicks and whirrs,
a doctor is saying something,
rattling off words
like a man jangling coins
in his pocket,
they are currency from a country
I have never been to
something on the films
cluster   mass
I am tripped by translation
something on the films
struggling to calculate
the exchange rate,
my hand on the receiver
gone cold from the water
it was cupping at the sink
five minutes before.

Outside, a new nickel of moon
is just rolling up from the trees.
Across a border, places are being set
for a dinner. I imagine the doctor
going home to his dinner.
I believe I even say thank you.
Everything ticks on as it has,

pulse, hour, season,
the unseemly swell in the new,
hard buttons of dogwood,
and the reddening evening sky
a metastasis of sun.

MAMMOGRAM

I made the mistake
of looking down—
breast coaxed away
from my chest to end
in a thinned-out puddle
of tissue, between plastic
clear as a grade-school petri dish,
some specimen pithed and opened,
suspended for view in a jar,
and all those playground
taunts come true,
flat, in fact,
as a pancake.

But the films clipped up later
in the doctor's light
transformed the world,
like the first satellite reports
of a visionary landscape,
celestial, sublunary,
nicked with grainy brilliance,
a curved, primitive planet
I floated, tethered,
proprietary, above.

Then *there* and *there,*
his offhand ballpoint
tapped like a miner
at the marvelous crust,
gauging the find,
the wedge of entry,
and I turned back

from the black-and-white
prospects of that surface
to the featureless scape
drawn out by machine,
saw it for what it might
easier, better, have been—
a cheek fast under ice,
or a face, hard
against a windshield.

Biopsy

Suddenly it is there
on its pogo-stick of sound,
like some bastard brother
out of Beatrix Potter—
Flopsy, Mopsy, and Biopsy.
You cannot shove it away.
It settles in
like the quality of light
in the sky.
It is not the door
but the heavy, brass knocker;
not the frost
but its first stark breath;
it is not the word
but the tongue that shapes it,
the language that nothing,
and everything, waits in,
the truth
of that shriveled meat
of rabbit's foot.

"I've been thinking of you,"
my sister says, meaning
she's been thinking of herself,
how this kernel in my body
might be hers, some rogue seed
hidden for years until stirred
to hunger, how our mothers
and grandmothers draw us
into this circle where the weight
of their fate closes like the iron grip
of a hand we cannot unclasp.

Now my sister watches me
in a new, bright way,
listens like a waiting inheritor,
as I, the sudden miser,
hoard my sack of breath,
measuring each word,
each act, each desire
like a coin against its cost
of effort—what is this worth?
what is this worth?
It is the shadow over the sun,
the thumb coming over the edge
of the blurred, imperfect
family picture.

IN DARK WEATHER

Tops of jack pines pitch
and lean, winds urging

their stiff, murmurous
curtsey to earth, swaying so far

I think they must simply
snap and give in

to the call of falling,
floating down in slow,

unstoppable motion, a marvel
of angle, the strict

hypotenuse of collapse,
how I see it all

happening, its end
before it ends,

and no startle,
or surprise,

just held curiosity
for the sounds that will come,

will I hear them in the house,
their trajectory threaten,

their path unnerve,
but somehow at the last

they pull back,
fan again into sky,

inscribing their arc in air
more liquid than light,

the high crenulations
of branches plying

a restless, distant surface.
Would I were certain

our natures were as charted,
that I knew what held

those columns safe at root,
yet still contained such threshing

in their reach, so might I
read the limits

of this weather,
the give in this torque

twisting us apart—
the fierce wind of anger,

the ice-lock of silence,
and *desire   desire*

the fall that shudders
every roof and story.

FLIGHT

It is what I've always wanted, you know,
found it first years back
in the mossy, haunted clearing
where the solo plane crashed
just missing our house and the schoolyard.
I'd cross the creosoted bridge
my father built from old telephone poles
when I was young, bone-thin,
crop-haired enough to be the boy
he always wanted, I'd crouch low
so my mother wouldn't know
I was turning upcreek, leaping
the lichened stones and pools,
slipping my shirt and my name
as easily as the shoes
she'd stiffly knotted,
setting course for the borderland
waiting in the shadows
of fugitive, forest light.

Later I'd find it sometimes
in the dark of rooms, or fields, in sex
and never with the right one,
some risk, some danger, you might say,
the little girl skipping school,
but that's too simple,
it was more in that poise,
the pure stepping through,
that place where I was flushed,
panting, the princess in torn velvet
who slammed shut the oven door herself,
or that doomed pilot

suspended in luminous loneliness,
all who might have saved us gone,
and only ourselves there to know
what had to be done
and I have done it,
and no one—this now with eyes
narrowed and fierce—
can know who I have been
or find where I have gone.

Above the bed the early evening sky
is violet, the color of shadows on snow.
I approach, and you are like glass,
no give in your surface,
blank as snowfield, distant as sky.
You might even be marble, so rigid
the line of your torso, throat.
In the rising moon, you will be lustrous,
I could marvel at the play
of silver on your skin,
not skin at all, but a luminous
envelope, the beaten leaf
of metalfoil, a translucent robe
of opal the heavens had flung down.
You will not stir as it covers you,
you will lie there, and become it,
sealed, remote, you
and the light and your shimmering
rightness, refusing to crack.
Why won't you forgive me,
why won't you slip?
I would grind your tears
into my hands
like needles of glass.

I have used up the easy love
there was and reached the weary,
long only to make an end.
It is more simple for you—
you sleep, you eat,
you work, say,
are you happy with him?
Happy   that word,
a beginner's word
like   *apple.*

You ask if he is afraid
I will leave him.
Would it pain you to know it is something
we never speak of, would it pain you
to know that *grocery*
mortgage   umbrella
come up in our quietest hours.
I have not once said,
save me   I am drowning
our whole life
is going under.

Young, you want to know
what is ahead.
Older, I never wish it,
know only how soon
my sons rise higher
and higher against my chest,
how tight the spiral inward feels,
the fall of innocence farther
and more lonely than I

had ever believed possible,
and I wonder about songs
that must play on
from the radios of cars
that have crashed through
the undulant gray of guardrails,
or into the flaring trees,
what that wild, ghostly music
must be like, playing out
over the odd, swooned bodies
as troopers and the curious
step cautiously up,
humming their quaint,
useless concerns.

MORNING AFTER

The carnival has ended, the circus left town,
the parade ground of pleasure and dare
returns to empty field. A rising quotidian
is slowly brooming shadows back from daybreak.
Here no ragged banners drag, no sentimental rain
rattles paint and wrappers.
Something simply was, and now isn't,
the eclipse of magical structure too common
and complete for grandeur.

When it is gone, we always turn home.
We know our fortune, the braille of our palms.
We never follow to the next town.
Like mercy, purpose, any love,
we are grateful it came at all,
that everything ordinary stopped,
that even the bronze frieze
of sanctified postures seemed to lift
from plinth and portico.

Now solitary walkers cross the grounds
where wind whips quicker unresisted,
and the negligent litter of random congregation
strews the flattened grass with torn,
shiny petals, but the sun shines only a shade
less bright, bells in a tower
do what bells always do,
and the courthouse flags shake out
like red bedsheets over the square.

The children are dreaming away.
They crouch in the next room,
the night is sorrow and wind.
I left their father years ago.

They crouch in the next room,
they take all I have.
I left their father years ago.
Silence is an old address.

They take all I have,
closed eyes and a heavy tongue.
Silence is an old address,
I keep secrets from everyone I love,

closed eyes and a heavy tongue,
so they will not leave me.
I keep secrets from everyone I love,
they give me gifts I do not deserve.

So they will not leave me
I make a trail. Only I know the way.
They give me gifts I do not deserve,
what am I to do with them all?

I make a trail, only I know the way.
I feed them with words, stitch them in tears,
what am I to do with them all?
I hoard what I can.

I feed them with words, stitch them in tears.
The night is sorrow and wind.
I hoard what I can.
The children are dreaming *away*.

MAPPAMUNDI

There were promises.
There were rings given and taken.
There were dreams and desires.
These were found in different places.
There were constellations
on the ceiling to steer by.
There were discoveries and disappearings,
there was slipping over the edge.
The intercession of angels was not unknown.
There were words and there was silence.
These were sometimes the same.
There were changes of costume
and their slow or hurried divestments.
There was frailty and saintliness.
There were years at sea,
and regrets, oh yes,
there were regrets.
There were intentions and consequences,
but they wore different names.
Always there were seasons,
time in the heart and time in the world.
These were not the same hours.
The city of god, as had been foretold,
was revealed at last
in the circumference
of the body miraculous,
wherefore there was rapture,
oh yes, there was rapture,
and no turning back
from that long falling
out of the sky.

III

THE ANGEL POEMS

Tell it, she said,
the Angel who sometimes
speaks to me,
and so I told
the only story I knew,
though I gave myself
another name.
You know the story, too,
but you know it
by another name.
That is the story.

TESSERAE, FOR GRIEF

Night and rain
are rumors
beyond me.
There is dirt
in my mouth.
A moon passes
in and out of clouds
like a sick eye
seeing,
not seeing.

✦

Seasons erase.
I rouse only to watch October
burn its red hour
through the world,
sink under again
beneath the slab of winter,
dreamless, white.
There is nothing to keep
in the layering
of days, nights,
mounding heavily over me.
Light and dark,
light and dark
take turns in a room
where my breath
and my body
used to open
and close.

✦

At first it is hard to pretend
to be alive. It gets easier.
No one really notices.
I have small boxes of time
to tell me when to stand,
to sit, to move a spoon.
When the drip of light pools
deep enough, it is morning.
When the throat of dark
drinks it back in,
it is night and I
unlock, fall over
like a spindle of blocks
a child has been trying
to balance all day.
I lie down and can be dead again.
It is good I do not have
to make the limp wings
of my lungs flutter,
or the fist of my heart
clench, clench.
Is this more than you want to know?
I am not talking to you,
or you. I am pretending
to talk to you.

✦

I remember a summer in another life,
smothered in the skin
that would spill my son,
how the heave and the heat,
the thick, scummed pool

my mind had seeped to,
would drown me in sleep so deep
I could not be raised.

Now, again, the hours slur,
the spur of sleep seeks me out,
or I coax after it, calling
sleep   sleep.
It is as if I am heavy with child again,
dragging the earth, month after month,
this great weight forcing the air
from my ribs, carving its cavity
into my heart. An incessant mouth
swells in my belly,
my bones are stretched to breaking.
My back is a stem
that never wanted to grow.

✦

I go down on all fours,
crawling down a hallway
where all the doors are shut.
I must find the one that opens
on a floor or a ditch
where I can finally lie down,
crying, finish it,
relinquish it,
let this pass out of me,
this stone,
this dead thing,
the terrible blood sac
of memory.

◆

I have been filled
and emptied,
filled and emptied,
until I am only a skin
crudely stitched
around hollows.
What can I ever hold again?

◆

The moon rims the clouds
like a discarded platter.
Old, cracked china,
how many women
have sighed up at you
and only seen
something more
to mend?

I feel you pulling me.
Soon it will be the blue flags,
and bloodroot along the creek,
then tulips with their
faint smell of celery.
I do not want them to touch me.
I want to curl back into winter,
the silence I am used to,
the sleep of sure steps.
It asks nothing of me.
I do not know what to do
when I walk outside
and the air fits me

with its cool sleeves.
That stir in the pines says
something is wanted,
something is wanted.
I want to turn back,
turn anywhere away
from this murmuring,
trembling, thrusting,
every stalk an arrow,
every petal a mouth,
pointing and calling.
I stand with this strange,
blank garment on my skin,
this raw, mutinous
life in my hands,
and I do not know how
to answer, or where
to start.

THE FIRST LESSON

The Angel knocked
and when I opened
the door to it
I lost the Angel
already sitting
at my table.
Wind poured in
through the crack
slapped my cheek
a voice cried   you cannot have
two Angels.
The Angel in the doorway said
let me in
I see
you are alone.

THE SECOND LESSON: DESIRE

You held me against
the side of the house
that faced the woods
where no one would see,
one hand holding my wrists,
your free hand lifting
my skirt as leaves
the color of burns
were breaking off and falling
through the barbed air
around us.
Memories of my dead
were all there in that season,
those I loved gone
deeper into the earth,
ash and flesh,
than any passion
into my skin,
and their faces
rose up to me
and the dark
my body cast me down
was where I might
grasp them at last,
giving over
felt that frightening
that free
that I cried out
when your grip
hauled me back,
your hand tangled
hard in my hair,

and I was turning,
coming back
into a day
where the sun
went on beating
red as a muscle.

THE THIRD LESSON: BETRAYAL

Let the wells
of our love
sicken

the forest
of our refuge
flame

let the fruit
of our desire
be as dust and barren

let there be
bitterness
anew with every sun

hatred
heralded
as rain

may the cradle
of our walls falter
and the seas writhe

may the moon
be riven
and the stars blister

and whatever sang
our joy
bite its tongue in two

and wail.

Why have you returned
under cover of dream
to this field of damage
where moonlight spreads
like the sheet
of an empty feast?
Are you foraging
for some word,
is there something
you wish back?
Have you come searching
for an answer
I have left you?
Wish it again.
I will tell you all.
I will tell you alone.
Seek it in the place of water,
seek it in the place of stones.
It is in the sky,
it is in the earth,
it is here, and here.
Overlook nothing.
We are the sum
of our secrets.

THE FIFTH LESSON: ABANDONMENT

And now I have lost
even this
little knowledge
of you and where
of an afternoon
you might let yourself
be found
I have lost
even this small imagining
of you and how
of a morning
very early
or very late
if I were blessed
I would see you
drawn up on your side
as if you were paused
in the climbing
of an invisible rope
and now I do not even know
where you are
or how I am
ever again to follow
the rope
and the light
you have pulled up
after you.

THE SIXTH LESSON: EXILE

This is the arctic of emotion.
It is as if I had fallen,
quick and burning,
through the center
of the earth, a black tunnel
of fire and salt

to finish here

where the world reaches away

blank   horizonless
a perfect   white circle   of ice
and erasure

my voice would have to travel so far
through such cold
on its thin chain of breath
it would feather down
in invisible crystals of silence

my own shadow
tethers me to this place

I curl in
a tight spiral
against myself
a nautilus
a little world

it does not matter
what way I turn

at the poles
of the earth
the only direction
is away

I see now
you are ordinary after all.
Your shape like my own,
your face simply a face,
its allotment of curves
and rises the same
as anyone's.
No temple of desire,
no noble mask.
You walked past
before I even realized
who you were.
To think once
when you turned
your face from me
I wanted to die.
I wanted to walk
off the earth
into the fall trees on fire,
into the last red mouth of the year,
where the sky was a field of carnage
and the sun going down
was the eye of a wild thing
dragging its blood spoor after it.

Now
again
your face.
Your ordinary face.
And the sky.
The ordinary sky.

Ignorance is all
that makes choice
possible.
To live
however blindly
is to choose.
Thus must it
always be
we learn
what we love
by what we lose.

THE ANGEL YET TO COME

What must it be like
to be without
the shawl of illusion,
to be past
all past consolations,
the difficult arts
of belief and blame,
to climb
by a means of falling,
a hauling up
of hands and voices,
unwinding the lifeline
that is scar and seam,
through years like rooms,
where to be motherless
is not to be unmothered,
and to be loved is not saved,
nor saved, spared
either burning bed or holy fire,
where truth is older, harder,
with no power to undo
and even bread is easier to share—
what must it be
ever to choose
without promise,
solace, or cease,
the stubborn stone
of the human.